My Thoughts

A Freewriting Journal

Janet Morey
Gail Schafers

PRO LINGUA ASSOCIATES

Dedication

to all our students, who over the years inspired us
to write this book

Contents

Pro Lingua Associates, Publishers
P.O. Box 1348
Brattleboro, Vermont 05302-1348 USA
Office: 802 257 7779
Orders: 800 366 4775
E-mail: orders@ProLinguaAssociates.com
SAN: 216-0579

Webstore: www.ProLinguaAssociates.com

Copyright © 2013 by Janet Morey and Gail Schafers

ISBN 13: 978-0-86647-350-7; 10: 0-86647-350-5

The book was set and designed by A.A. Burrows using Adobe's Times New Roman, a variant of one of the most popular type faces of the modern era. Originally it was created for *The Times* of London in 1931 by Victor Lardent and Stanley Morison. Its history is complicated and litigious. Linotype, working with *The Times*, registered it as Times Roman; Monotype, which originally issued the type, called it Times New Roman. Microsoft, Apple, and Adobe all have digital variants. All the variations are strong, easy-to-read serif fonts. The design of the cover uses a photograph of Blue Denim © Alfonsodetomas from Dreamstime. com. Other photos from that agency are, on page 48, purse, © Badahos, and on page 62, coffee, © Feng Yu. The design for the text was done in close collaboration with the authors.

This book was printed and bound by Edwards Brothers Malloy in Ann Arbor, Michigan.

Printed in the United States
First printing 2013. 2000 copies in print.

How do you feel on a rainy day?

What will you do with an empty box?

What color would you give
to your day yesterday?
Begin, "Yesterday my day was [gray] because…"

When you open a window at home in the morning,
what do you hear? Or
When you open a window at night,
what do you hear?
How does that make you feel?

Describe the happiest – or the friendliest –
person you know.

6

You are going to cook a special meal
for someone. Describe what it will be
and how to prepare it.

What is your opinion of pets?

8

Describe your feelings on your
first day of school as a child – or as an adult.

What do you need for a happy life?

10

What do you love most
about your favorite season?

Does a sunny day make you happy?
Does a gloomy day make you sad?
Answer one of these questions,
and explain your emotions.

Poet Carl Sandburg wrote,
"The fog comes
on little cat feet."
Why does Sandburg say this?
How would you describe fog?

A classmate will volunteer to be a model.
You are an artist, but instead of using
brushes and a palette,
you will work with pencil (or pen) and
<u>words</u> to "paint"
a portrait of your classmate.

14

Describe one of your favorite relatives.

Think about the many ways
you use water each day.
Write about how you can change what you do
to conserve water.

16

How did you help someone recently?
Or How did someone help you?

Write about your favorite plaything
when you were little.

What important lesson did you learn
from a teacher?

What language do you want to learn
next? Why?

20

In "Dreams," Poet Langston Hughes wrote,

> *"Hold fast to dreams*
> *For if dreams die*
> *Life is a broken-winged bird*
> *That cannot fly…"*

Explain your dreams for the future.

Write about the first friend you ever had.
Tell what you did together.

Describe an adventure you
would like to have.

Do you enjoy competition?
Why, or why not?
How you do feel when you win?
How do you feel when you lose?

Write an ice cream memory.

"Today is the tomorrow you worried about yesterday."

Author Unknown

What things do you worry about?

What do you *see*, *hear*, and *smell*
when you walk along a beach?

Or

What do you *see, hear,* and *smell*
when you walk in the woods in autumn?

What is something you dislike, such as
being alone at night or taking a school exam
or seeing the dentist…
or spiders or bees?
Give reasons for your choice.

If you can do anything you want
all day tomorrow, what will you do?

Everyone likes to be alone sometimes.
Children choose a tree house, a fort, a closet.
Adults escape to a garden, a library,
a corner in a coffee house.
Where do you go?

30

How did you feel
when you first climbed a tree
or
when you first rode a bicycle?

Poet Billy Collins chooses "Morning"
as the best part of the day:

"This is the best—
throwing off the light covers,
feet on the cold floor,
and buzzing around the house on espresso—"

Write about your favorite time of the day, and tell why.

You just won the lottery!
What will you do with ALL that money?

How do you react when the sky
turns black and thunder roars?

34

What is your remedy for a nasty cold?

Describe eating an apple,
from first delicious bite to last.

Describe an old person you know.

Daisies are thought to be common;
roses are thought to be elegant.
Which are you, a daisy or a rose? Why?
Or Are you another kind of flower?

Most ducks fly south in the fall.
Imagine that you are a duck.
Where will you fly to, and why?

Poet A. A. Burrows writes
about *"The Porcupine."*

*"...I met him sitting in a tree.
I looked at him. He looked at me.
I said to him, 'How do you do?'
With bright, black eyes he looked me through.
It then occurred to him to flee
by climbing slowly up the tree."*

Write about your favorite wild animal. Or
Create a poem about your favorite wild animal.

What is your favorite game?
How do you play it?

What smell do you remember from your past?

What do you enjoy most about a visit to a zoo?

Write about something you did with your mother
or grandmother
when you were younger.

What do you grab for a snack
after school?
Is this important for your day?

No two blades of grass – or snowflakes –
or people – are exactly the same.
How are *you* different from anyone else?

46

What is your favorite food?
What is your least favorite food?
Clearly describe the *taste* of each.

Define loneliness.
When have you felt lonely?
What did you do about it?

Describe something that you found.
Imagine who lost it and how it was lost.

People often complain about the weather:
"It's too hot." Or *"It's too cold."*
Tell what you LIKE about hot days or cold days.

What is (or was) your favorite
room in your home?
Why?

Describe the smells of summer.
Or Describe the smells of winter.

English poet Emily Bronte wrote,
"Every leaf speaks bliss to me
Fluttering from the autumn tree."

Imagine that you are an autumn leaf,
"fluttering" from a tall tree.
What do you see and feel?

Do you enjoy soaking
in a bathtub? Or
Do you prefer taking
a hot shower?

In "Ode to My Socks," Chilean poet Pablo Neruda
wrote:

"... The moral of my ode is this:
beauty is twice beauty...
and what is good is doubly good
when it is a matter of two socks
made of wool in winter."

Write anything that comes to mind about *socks*.

You receive a package in the mail.
What's inside? Who is it from?

When I hear the song, _____,
I always feel _____.

Poet A. A. Burrows shows the beauty of an ice storm:

"The radio warned of rain.
And then the world suddenly turned all glass.
We gasped at this new beauty, so strange,
unexpected, unreal."

Describe something beautiful in the natural world.

Describe a windy day and
how it makes you *feel*.

You want to sell this car.
What will you say to
persuade someone to buy it?

You have been chosen to take a journey into space,
and you are on your way!
What do you see, hear, and feel as you lift off?

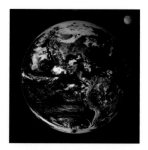

Describe the perfect job for you.

Define bullying.
If you see a bully picking on someone,
what will you do about it, and why?

64

Imagine that your uncle offered to buy you
your dream car.
You went to the dealer yesterday.
Describe your choice in detail.

If you could choose to be: invisible
or super strong
or able to read people's minds,
which would you choose, and why?

Which is your favorite sport
to play—or to watch?
Explain your answer.

You are going for a run around your neighborhood.
You leave your front door and turn to the right.
Describe what you see on your route.

You are planning
to take a motorcycle trip
through your country.
Where would you travel, and why?

You looked out your bedroom window this morning
and saw—a dinosaur!—in your neighbor's yard.
How did you feel, and what did you do?

Your friend is thinking of getting a tattoo,
and she wants your advice.
Tell her your opinion of tattoos.

Many children and adults spend hours and hours,
day and night at the computer.
Are you one of them? How do you feel about this?

Do texting and social media (Facebook and twitter)
have more good points or more bad points?
What has happened to face-to-face conversations?

"I fear the day when technology will surpass our human interaction."

Albert Einstein

Technology makes cheating easier than ever before.
Is cheating ever okay? Give your opinion.

What are your thoughts
now on freewriting?

.

More of my thoughts

More of my thoughts

More of my thoughts

More of my thoughts

More of my thoughts

More of my thoughts

A last thought

How do you feel on a rainy day? • 1

What will you do with an empty box? • 2

What color would you give to your day yesterday?   • 3

When you open a window at home, what do you hear? • 4

Describe the happiest person you know. • 5

You are going to cook a special meal for someone. • 6

What is your opinion of pets? • 7

Describe your feelings on your first day of school. • 8

What do you need for a happy life? • 9

What do you love most about your favorite season? • 10

Does a sunny day make you happy? • 11

Carl Sandburg: *Fog* • 12

A classmate will volunteer to be a model. • 13

Describe one of your favorite relatives. • 14

Think about the various ways you use water each day. • 15

How did you help someone recently? • 16

Write about your favorite plaything when you were little. • 17

What important lesson did you learn from a teacher? • 18

What language do you want to learn next? • 19

Langston Hughes: *Dreams* • 20

Write about the first friend you ever had. • 21

Describe an adventure you would like to have. • 22

Do you enjoy competition? • 23

Write an ice cream memory. • 24

What things do you worry about? • 25

What do you *see, hear,* and *smell* walking on a beach or in the woods? • 26

What is something you dislike? • 27

If you can do anything you want tomorrow, what will you do? • 28

Everyone likes to be alone sometimes. • 29

How did you feel when you first climbed a tree? • 30

Billy Collins: *Morning* • 31

You just won the lottery! • 32

How do you react when the sky turns black? • 33

What is your remedy for a nasty cold? • 34

Describe eating an apple. • 35

Describe an old person you know. • 36

Daisies are thought to be common. • 37

Most ducks fly south in the fall. • 38

A.A. Burrows: *The Porcupine* • 39

What is your favorite game? • 40

What smell do you remember from your past? • 41

What do you enjoy most about a visit to a zoo? • 42

Write about something you did with your mother. • 43

What do you grab for a snack after school? • 44

No two blades of grass are exactly the same. • 45

What is your favorite food? • 46

Define loneliness. • 47

Describe something that you found. • 48

People often complain about the weather. • 49

What is your favorite room in your home? • 50

Describe the smells of summer. • 51

Emily Bronte: *Every leaf speaks bliss to me* • 52

Why are people afraid of snakes? • 53

Do you enjoy soaking in a bathtub? • 54

Pablo Neruda: *Ode to My Socks* • 55

You receive a package in the mail. • 56

When I hear the song, ___, I always feel ___. • 57

A.A. Burrows: *The Ice Storm* • 58

Describe a windy day and how it makes you feel. • 59

You want to sell this car. • 60

You have been chosen to take a journey into space. • 61

Describe the perfect job for you. • 62

Define bullying. • 63

Imagine that your uncle offered to buy you your dream car. • 64

If you could choose to be invisible... • 65

Which is your favorite sport to play or watch? • 66

You are going for a run around your neighborhood. • 67

You are planning to take a motorcycle trip. • 68

You looked out your window this morning and saw a dinosaur! • 69

Your friend is thinking of getting a tattoo. • 70

Many children and adults spend hours and hours at the computer. • 71

Do social media have more good points or more bad points? • 72

Technology makes cheating easier than ever before. • 73

What are your thoughts now on freewriting? • 74

More of my thoughts • 75

More of my thoughts • 76

More of my thoughts • 77

More of my thoughts • 78

More of my thoughts • 79

More of my thoughts • 80

A last thought • 81

Index of Prompts